MEGA MASH-UP

Secret Agents in the Jungle

Nikalas Catlow
Tim Wesson

Draw your own adventure!

nosy crow

Mega Mash-Up: Secret Agents v Giant Slugs in the Jungle

Published in the UK in 2012 by Nosy Crow Ltd
The Crow's Nest
10a Lant Street
London, SE1 1QR, UK

A CIP catalogue record for this book is available from the British Library

ISBN: 978 0 85763 103 9
Printed in China

This book needs

you!

Your hand

What if some tiny SLUGS fell into a pool of **toxic** goo and became Giant Slugs?

What if some **Secret Agents** were sent into the JUNGLE to check it out?

Would the Giant Slugs :TAKE OVER THE WORLD?:

Or would the Secret Agents vanquish them with their deadly weapon?

You'll have to finish the illustrations and find out...

Prepare to **LAUGH** while you doodle and SNIGGER while you read.

Slime Sucker

Introducing the Secret Agents!

Gadget Gavin

Secret Steve

Agent X

Dangerous Dave

Cryptic Carl

INTRODUCING the Giant Slugs!

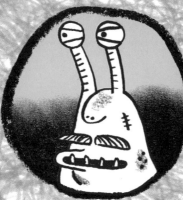

Sticky Colin

Big Suzy

Slime Ball

Gloop

Oozy Bob

You'll need these...

drawing tools

These are the **3** tools that Nikalas and Tim have used to create the artwork in this book.

felt-tip pen or marker

pencil

wax crayon

PEN

crayon

Using different tools helps create great drawings

texture page

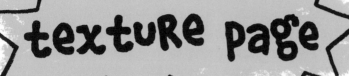

pen zigzags

crayon rubbing from lino floor

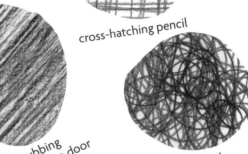

cross-hatching pencil

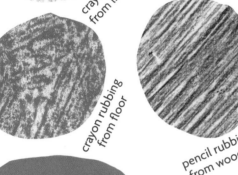

crayon rubbing from floor

pencil rubbing from wooden door

scribbly pencil

There are loads of ways you can add texture to your artwork. Here are a few examples

crayon rubbing from wall

pencil dashes

pen circles

DRAWING TIP!
Turn to the back of the book for ideas on stuff you might want to draw in this adventure

Chapter 1

A Toxic Goo Brew...

Add woody texture to the trees

Add JUNK to this heap

An OIL COMPANY has been drilling in the Jungle and left it in a right old mess.
Two workers are supposed to be cleaning up.
But the Jungle is creepy and they are getting SPOOKED...

Draw a ferocious bear!

Suddenly, a twig SNAPS and out
of the undergrowth comes a **HUGE BEAR**!
The scaredy-cat workers FLEE IN PANIC, leaving an
overturned barrel dripping **toxic goo** into a
strange-looking pool...

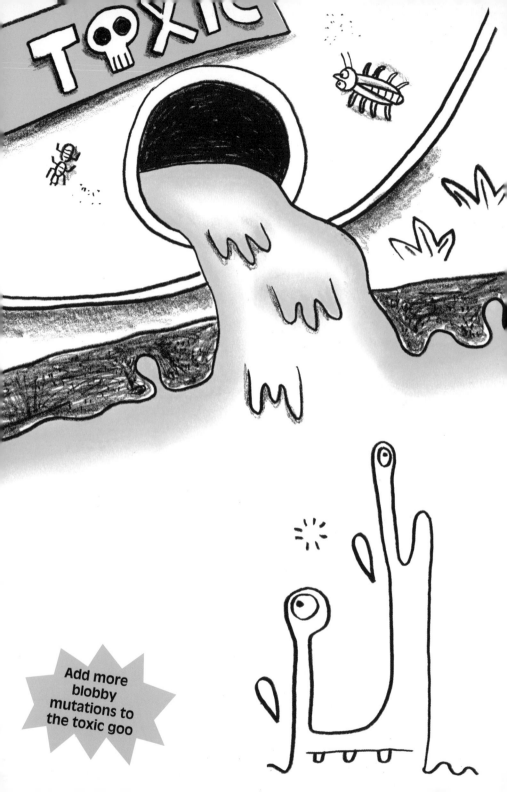

Draw a slug doing backstroke

Some small slugs slither curiously towards
the foul-smelling pool. But OOPS, they slip-slide in!
The slime **bubbles** furiously...

Draw your own evil
GIANT SLUG!

One Giant Slug declares
himself leader.

"I am **SLiMe BaLL**," he roars, crazed with
ambition. "Who wants to join me and
 TAKE OVER THE WORLD?"

Design a
poster for
Slime Ball's
evil gang!

"We do!" cry four revoltingly ugly Giant Slugs. "And we will use our new super-weapon: TOXIC SNOT!"

"World domination here we come!" cackles Slime Ball.
"And **NO ONE** can stop us..."

Chapter 2

Operation Slime Time

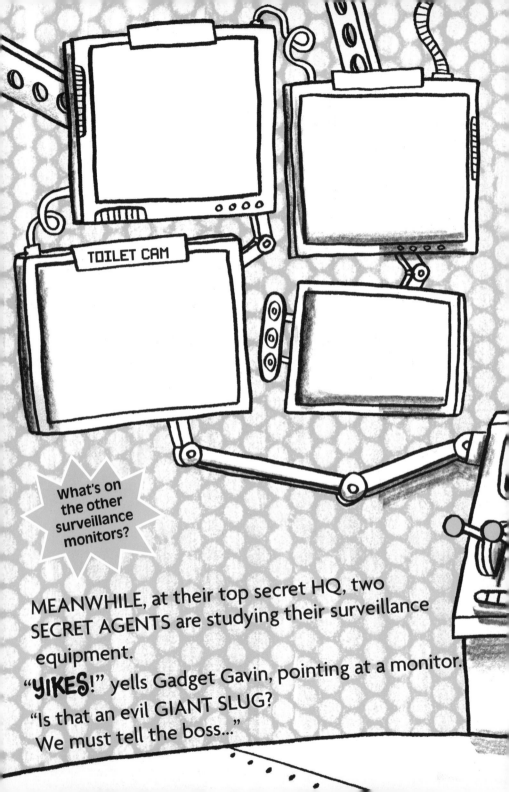

TOILET CAM

What's on the other surveillance monitors?

MEANWHILE, at their top secret HQ, two SECRET AGENTS are studying their surveillance equipment.

"**YIKES!**" yells Gadget Gavin, pointing at a monitor.

"Is that an evil GIANT SLUG? We must tell the boss..."

Agent X assembles a crack team to investigate the Jungle.
"These boys have seen more Jungle action than I've had hot dinners!" he says.
"Prepare for Operation Slime Time!"

You wouldn't want to get into a fight with him!

PROFILE

NAME: AGENT X

EXPERTISE:

HOBBIES:

COMBAT STYLE:

NAME: DANGEROUS DAVE

EXPERTISE: SKY DIVING WITHOUT A PARACHUTE BEHIND ENEMY LINES.

HOBBIES: BASE JUMPING IN A WING SUIT, KUNG FU WITH A BLINDFOLD, MOTOR RACING IN A BURNING CAR, CROCHET AND POTTERY.

COMBAT STYLE: KAMIKAZE

NAME: CRYPTIC CARL

EXPERTISE:

HOBBIES:

COMBAT STYLE:

NAME: SECRET STEVE

EXPERTISE:

HOBBIES:

COMBAT STYLE:

NAME: GADGET GAVIN

EXPERTISE:

HOBBIES:

COMBAT STYLE:

Fill in the profile sheets

Deep in the basement, Gadget Gavin and his team are inventing more **top secret gadgets**.
"Ooh, careful with that RAY GUN!"

ZAP!

Fill the laser cupboard

YUCK! What's his head turned into?

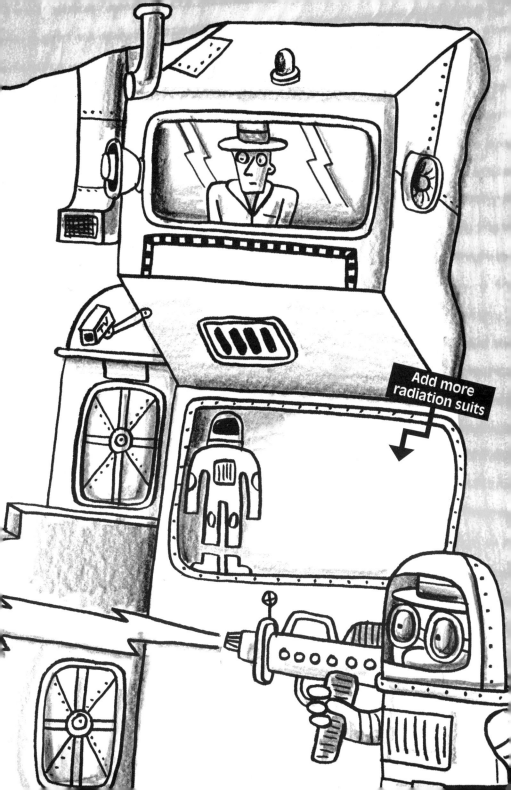

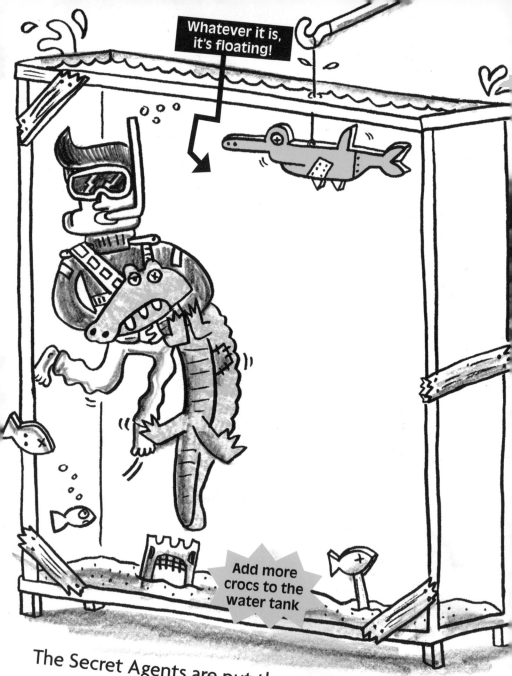

The Secret Agents are put through a punishing **training regime** in a controlled "Jungle environment". "OK men, pack your bags," says Agent X. "We fly to the Jungle tonight."

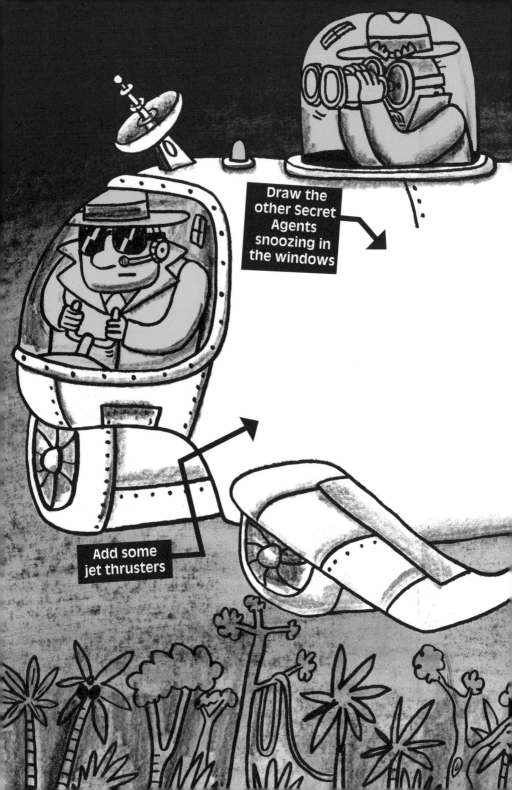

The **CRACK TEAM** of Secret Agents board their crack plane. "Let's go BUST SOME SLUGS," cries Cryptic Carl.

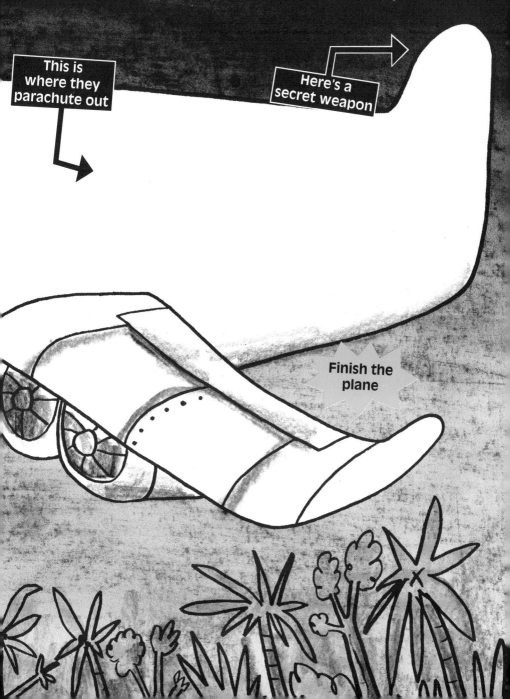

This is where they parachute out

Here's a secret weapon

Finish the plane

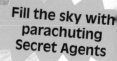

Check out that cloud surfing!

The SECRET AGENTS land **BEHIND ENEMY LINES**.
It's time for a rumble in the jungle

Chapter 3

Lights!
Camera!
Action!

The SECRET AGENTS build their base camp **in the tree tops**. "I'm the King of the Swingers, yeah!" laughs Dangerous Dave.

Agent X frowns. "Stop monkeying around!"

Here's a helicopter on a landing pad

Finish the Secret Agents' tree-top base camp

"Keep down, Carl," whispers Agent X.

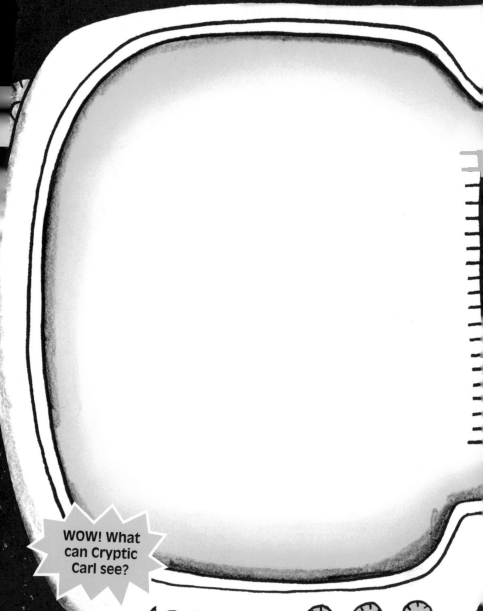

WOW! What can Cryptic Carl see?

"CRIPES!" exclaims Cryptic Carl, peering through his night-vision goggles. "What on EARTH is that?"

What is Oozy Bob thinking about?

Give oozy texture to Oozy Bob

The Giant Slugs go into make-up and the Director talks them through scene one. "Attack everyone, and take over the world!" he says.

"It'll be like a practice run," chuckles Slime Ball, slimily.

What strange costume is Sticky Colin wearing?

"ACTION!" shouts the Director. The Giant Slugs go beserk! **CRUNCH! SLURP! MUNCH!** They're EATING the film crew!

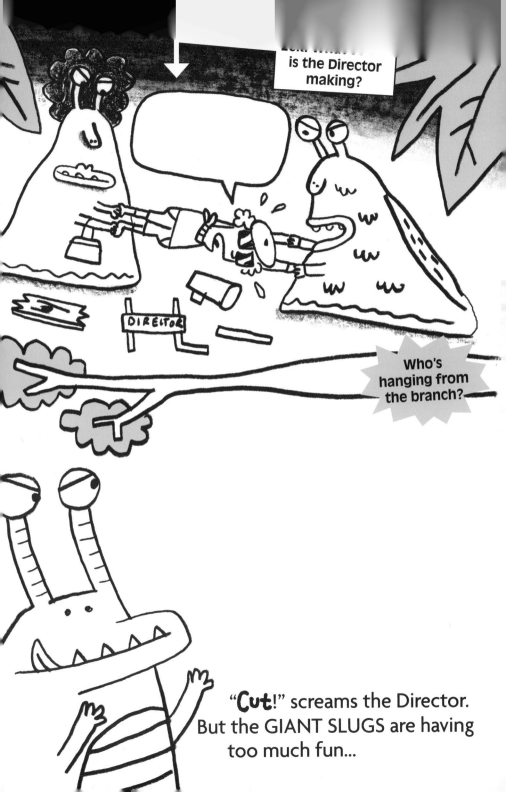

IMMOBILIZER 1000

Give the Immobilizer 1000 more buttons and levers

WHOOSH! Down comes the net and Oozy Bob is trapped!

Draw Oozy Bob wriggling in the net!

Chapter 4

THERE'S something ODD About Oozy Bob

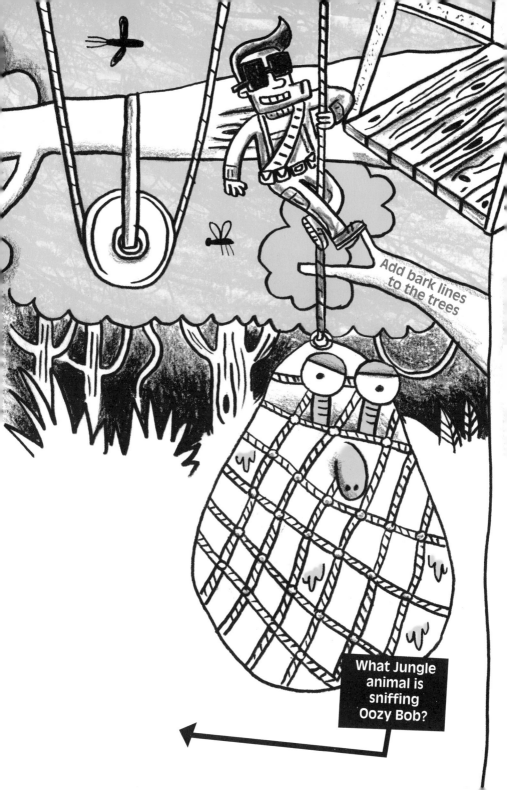

The Secret Agents strap Oozy Bob to their
Fact-Extractor...
"What's your EVIL PLAN, Giant Slug?" demands Agent X

"**Schlerrrp!**" replies Oozy Bob.

"That's a rubbish plan," points out Gadget Gavin.

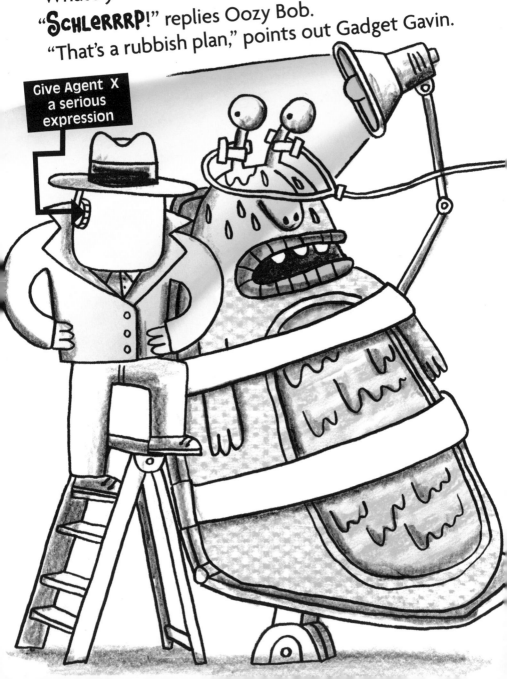

Give Agent X a serious expression

Finish the SECRET AGENTS' Fact-Extractor

The interrogation starts and Cryptic Carl bombards Oozy Bob with questions.
"Why do you smell so bad?" he quizzes. "Do you eat your own bogeys?"
But Oozy Bob won't talk . . .

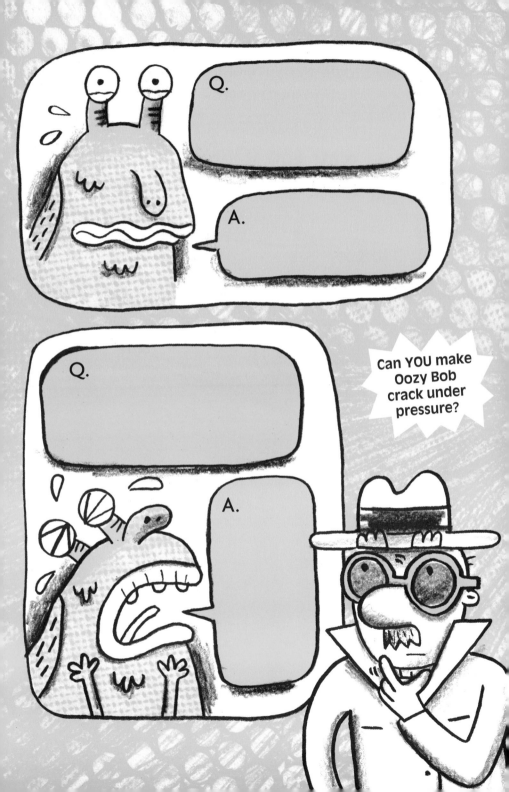

"Oh, this is useless!" yells Agent X. "Bring in the Slug Decoy machine! We'll INFILTRATE their slimy gang IN DISGUISE."

"Can I drive it?" asks Dangerous Dave, excitedly.

"No! **You're WAY too Dangerous,**" replies Agent X. "You get the back end!"

At Camp Slug, the evil gang is studying the PLAN OF ACTION when the Slug Decoy machine rumbles in.

Add some doodles to illustrate the plan!

Plan to invade THE CITY and take over world...

1. Rampage into city

2. Have a hair cut and then eat the hairdresser

3. Slime a bus-load of people

Add texture and shading to the Giant Slugs

"Oozy Bob!" says Sticky Colin. "Where you been, man?"
He does a double-take . . . "You're not Oozy Bob!
Attack, attack!"

4. Gobble the Queen of England

5. Terrorise lots more people

6. Declare the world ours!

What does the Secret Agents' radio look like?

"**Mayday, Mayday!**" Agent X radios back to the other Secret Agents. "We've been **Rumbled**, we'll have to make a run for it!"

Chapter 5
Slugs
Rule the
WORLD

The SECRET AGENTS make a run for it but the Slug Decoy machine slows them down and the GIANT SLUGS are right behind. "Destroy them!" spits Slime Ball.

Finish the rope-bridge maze!

The Slug Decoy machine smashes to pieces as the SECRET AGENTS fall into a pit of crocodiles.

Thank goodness for their crocodile-wrestling training! **SNAP! SNAP!**

Fill the pit
with HUNGRY
crocodiles!

All the Secret Agents at the base can hear are snapping sounds and screaming. "**THAT DOESN'T SOUND GOOD**," says Gadget Gavin. "Thank heavens I've been working on Plan B."

Meanwhile, the Giant Slugs are back at Camp Slug and packing for their trip to THE CITY.
"What should I wear to take over the world?" ponders Big Suzy.
"I'm gonna eat a **Lot of HumaNS**," laughs Slime Ball.

Finish this map of THE CITY

MAP

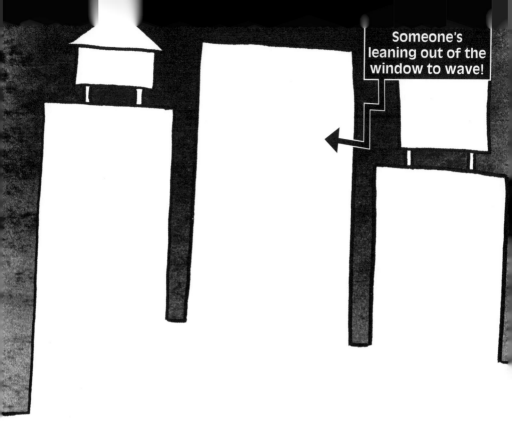

Someone's leaning out of the window to wave!

The GIANT SLUGS soon reach the bright lights of THE CITY. Big Suzy starts **DROOLING** at the thought of getting a trendy new haircut and sliming all those humans!

The Giant Slugs **DESCEND** on THE CITY . . .

You write the scene!

Chapter 6

Exploding Slugs!

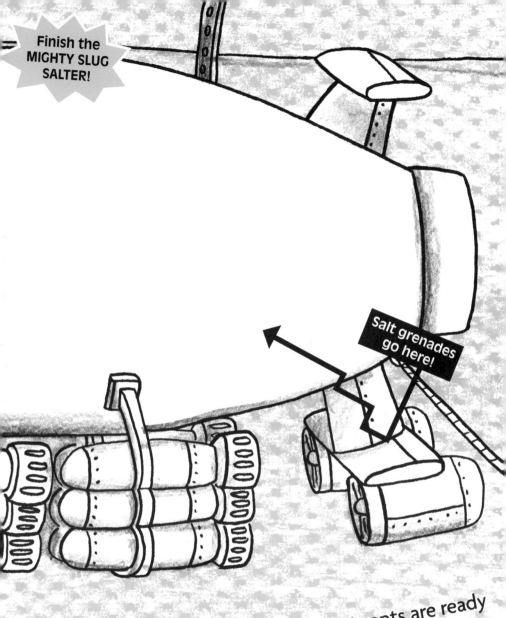

Meanwhile back in the Jungle, the Secret Agents are ready for action. "**The Mighty Slug Salter is complete!**" cries Gadget Gavin. "Let the SALT ASSAULT begin!"

The **ENORMOUS ZEPPELIN** flies silently through the sky.
"The enemy has been sighted," cries Agent X.
"OK, boys, GET READY TO SLUG this one out!"

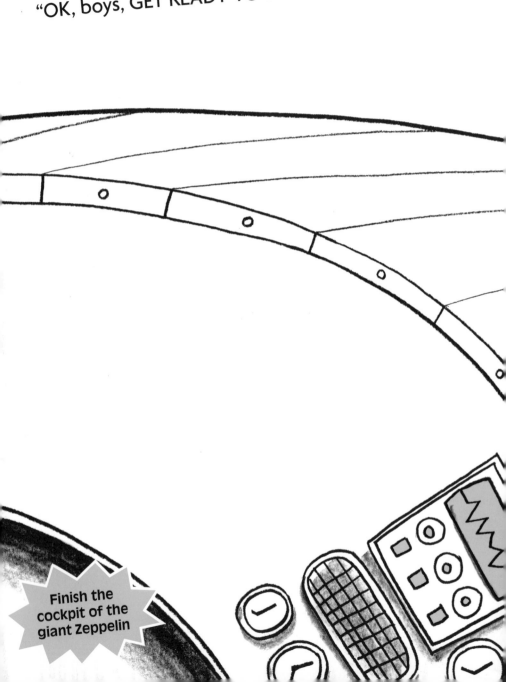

Finish the cockpit of the giant Zeppelin

"**Giant Slugs at ten o'clock!**" cries Agent X.
"Engage the **Brine Cannons!** SALT BOMBS AWAY!"

BOOM!

BOOM!

What's happening on the roof?

Soon the sky is raining salty water. The salt makes the Giant Slugs' toxic slime **fizz** dangerously and...

BOOM!

Who else is on the bridge?

POP! SPLAT! The Giant Slugs **EXPLODE!**
All the slimy monsters leave behind are little
puddles of ooze.

POP!

What does
Slime Ball look
like when
he explodes?

SQUELCH

YUCK! Sticky Colin has turned inside out!

EXPLODE those Evil GIANT SLUGS!

Who else is cheering in the crowd?

"HURRAH!"

Slugmania is no more. The Secret Agents have saved the world from Giant Slugs!

HOW I INFILTRATED THE SLUG CAMP
by Dangerous
Draw the Slug Decoy machine
A STICK
END
Draw the mighty SLUG SALTER

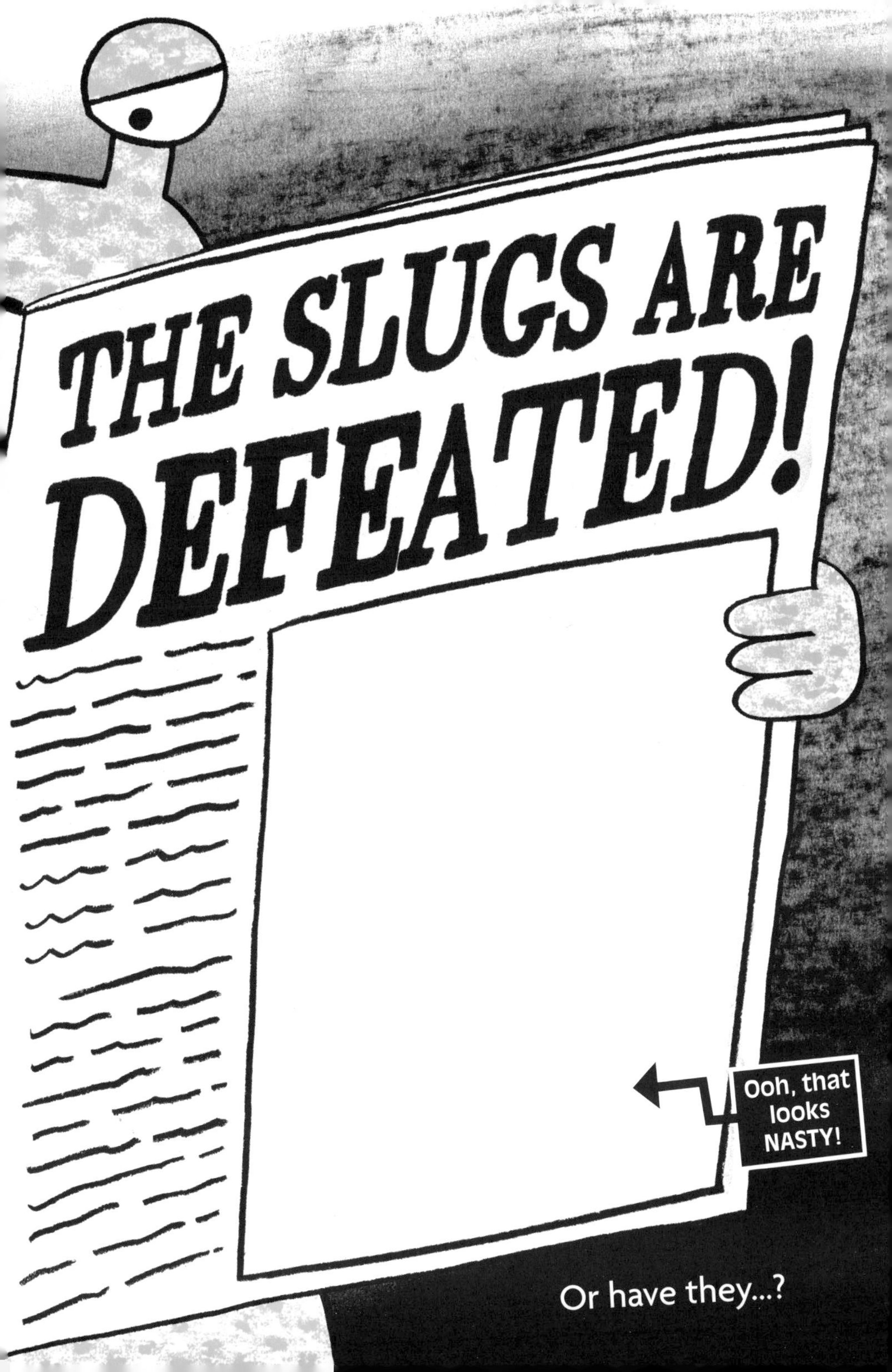
THE SLUGS ARE DEFEATED!
Ooh, that looks NASTY!
Or have they...?

Picture Glossary

If you get stuck or need ideas, then use these pages for reference.

Bridge

Secret Agents' Treehouse bits

Radio mast

Look-out post

Communications tower

Parachuting Agents

If you like, you can copy the pictures. OR you can draw your own version.

Bits of Junk

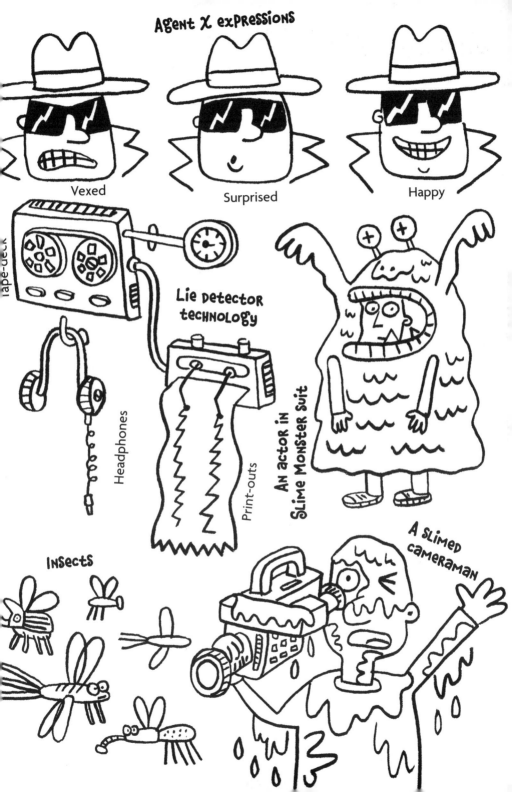

Agent X expressions

Vexed

Surprised

Happy

Tape-deck

Lie detector technology

Headphones

Print-outs

An actor in Slime Monster suit

A slimed cameraman

Insects

Picture Glossary

If you get stuck or need ideas, then use these pages for reference.

Jet Thruster

Secret Agent Plane gadgets

Dials and Meters

Artillery

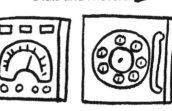

Shrink Ray

Squash Ray

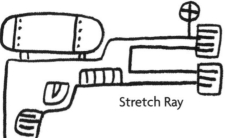

Stretch Ray

If you like, you can copy the pictures. OR you can draw your own version.

Visit our **AWESOME** website and get involved!

Website

www.megamash-up.com
Upload artwork and get the latest news

Also available